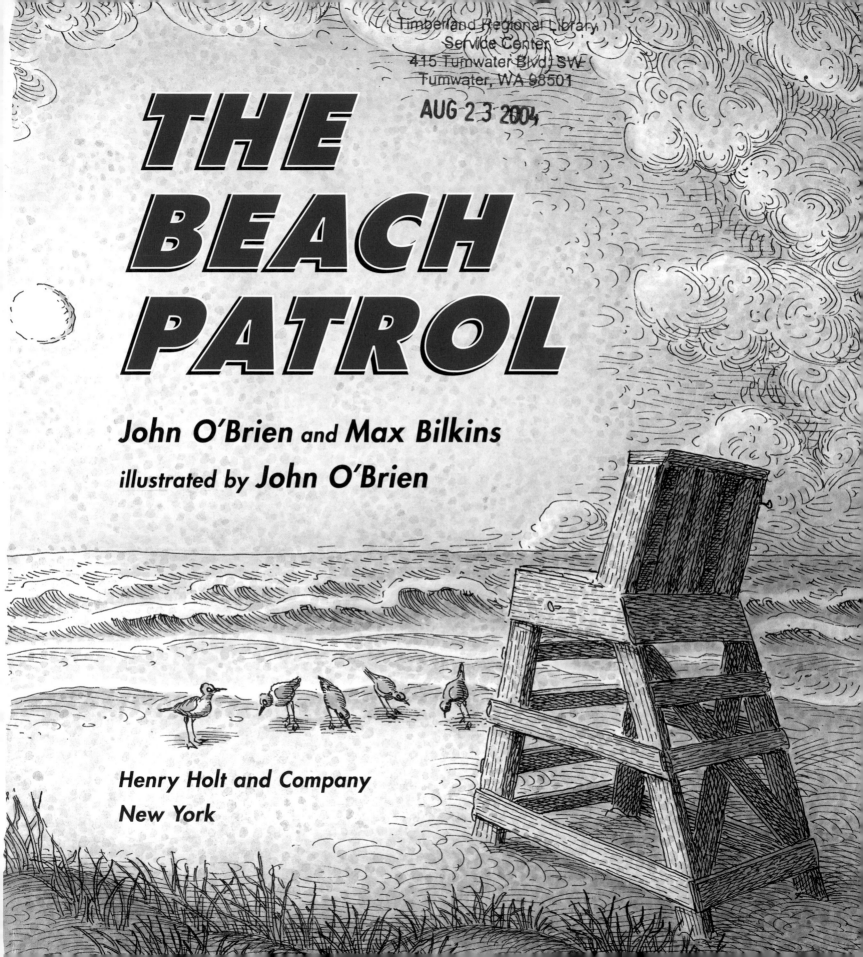

THE BEACH PATROL

John O'Brien and Max Bilkins

illustrated by John O'Brien

Henry Holt and Company
New York

Henry Holt and Company, LLC
Publishers since 1866
115 West 18th Street, New York, New York 10011
www.henryholt.com

Henry Holt is a registered trademark of Henry Holt and Company, LLC
Text copyright © 2004 by John O'Brien and Max Bilkins
Illustrations copyright © 2004 by John O'Brien
All rights reserved.
Distributed in Canada by H. B. Fenn and Company Ltd.

Library of Congress Cataloging-in-Publication Data
O'Brien, John.
The beach patrol / by John O'Brien and Max Bilkins; illustrated by John O'Brien.
Summary: Describes the beach patrol's typical day on a crowded beach,
including the equipment, terminology, characteristics of the ocean, and
behavior of beach goers with which a lifeguard must be familiar.
1. Lifeguards—Juvenile literature. [1. Lifeguards. 2. Occupations.] I. Bilkins, Max. II. Title.
GV838.72.O37 2004   797.2′1′0284—dc22   2003012246
ISBN 0-8050-6911-9 / First Edition—2004 / Designed by Donna Mark
Printed in the United States of America on acid-free paper. ∞
1 3 5 7 9 10 8 6 4 2

The artist used watercolor on bristol paper
to create the illustrations for this book.

To my daughter, Tess, and all the guards of the North Wildwood
and South Jersey beach patrols with whom I've had the pleasure
of sharing many great summers.
—J. O'B.

To my wife, Sandra, and my daughters, Nicole, Tara, and Brianna,
for their everlasting support and encouragement; they truly know
how much working "on the beach" means to me. To Dave, thank you
for being a best friend and for all of your input toward this book.
To the Wildwood Crest Beach Patrol for allowing me the experience
of being a part of one of the finest beach patrols anywhere.
Thank you.
—M. B.

VROOM!

It's 6 A.M. and the beach crew is getting ready for a big weekend crowd. The day begins with raking, scraping, shoveling, sifting, and poking. The sand will be clean and smooth by the time the workers are finished.

Load and Pack
picks up trash and
recyclable containers.

Surf Rake
rakes up large items,
like bottles, cans,
and towels.

Surf Clam

ROLL CALL!

Sanitizer
picks up paper and smaller items.

Sifter
strains the sand to pick out
the smallest trash.

Laughing Gull

Many lifeguards call their headquarters the "tent" because years ago it really was a tent.

BEACH PATROL RANK

Chief

Captain

Lieutenant

Driver

Lifeguard

Rookie (first-year guard)

The flag is raised at 9:30 sharp. Members of the beach patrol arrive at the "tent" for duty.

"*Roll call*," shouts the captain.

The lieutenants make sure the guards know where they will be posted for the day.

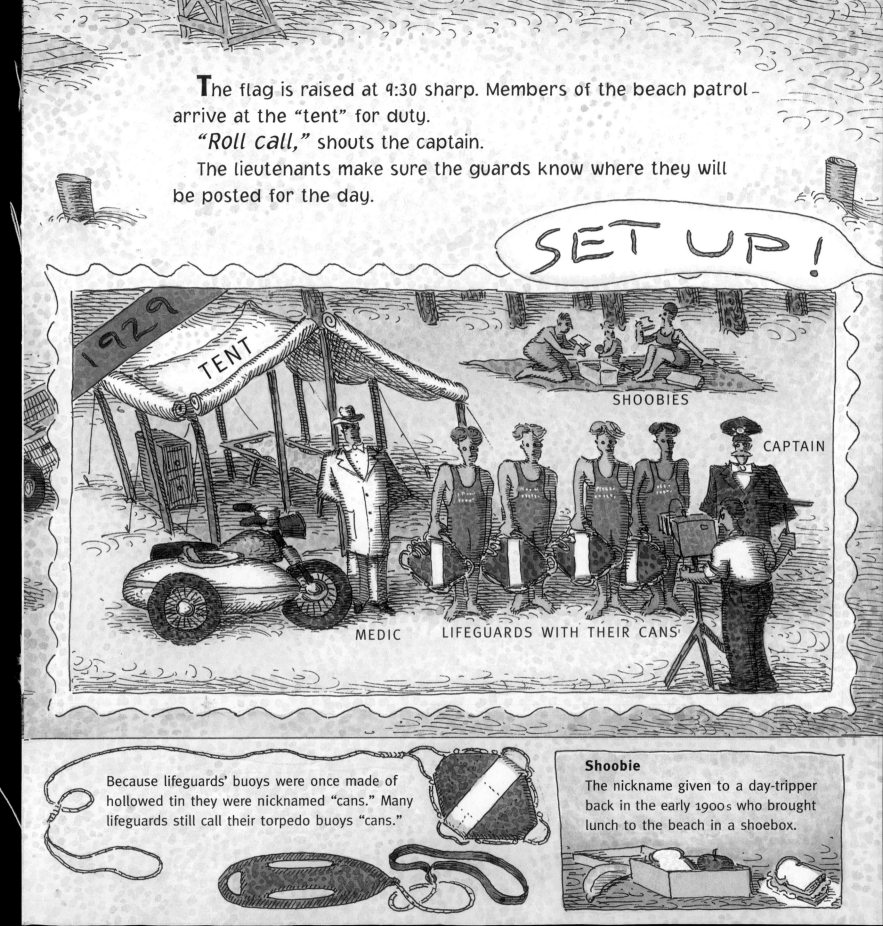

SET UP!

1929

TENT

SHOOBIES

CAPTAIN

MEDIC

LIFEGUARDS WITH THEIR CANS

Because lifeguards' buoys were once made of hollowed tin they were nicknamed "cans." Many lifeguards still call their torpedo buoys "cans."

Shoobie
The nickname given to a day-tripper back in the early 1900s who brought lunch to the beach in a shoebox.

Lanyard and Whistle

Toeboard

First Aid Kit

Torpedo Buoy (Torp)

Hat

"Grab your gear and git!"
"Hustle down!"

The guards head for their stands, loaded up with everything they might need for the day. Some walk; a few lucky ones get a ride.

Umbrella

Sweats

Uniform

Water Jug

Sunglasses

Sunscreen

Pocket Mask (a CPR rescue breathing device)

When the lifeguards reach their "streets," they drag their stands from the soft sand to the water's edge, where they can be closest to the bathers.

Beachgoers begin to arrive and pick their favorite spots to set up.

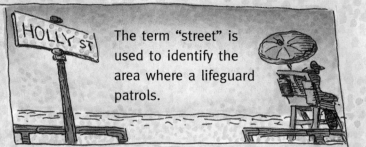

The term "street" is used to identify the area where a lifeguard patrols.

Tide Facts
- Tides change about every 6 hours and 15 minutes.
- The most extreme high and low tides occur farthest from the equator.

STAND
Seat
Can Nail
Toeboard
Rungs

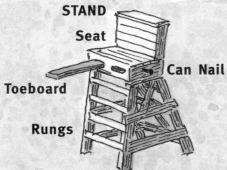

Sitting Wood
Lifeguard slang for sitting up on the stand.

Jetty: A man-made formation of rock, cement, or other materials to prevent beach erosion or to protect harbors from the open seas.

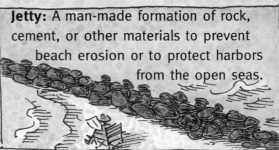

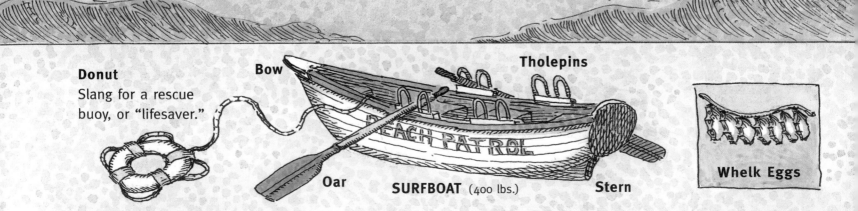

By midday, the ocean is very crowded. The guards keep their "stands wet" to stay close to the bathers as they watch their water. Heads swivel: left, front, right. Boat layout, can layout, paddleboard.

Some lifeguards also watch their bathers from the water.

Donut
Slang for a rescue buoy, or "lifesaver."

Bow

Tholepins

Oar

SURFBOAT (400 lbs.)

Stern

Whelk Eggs

"**B**ack beach," in the soft sand, there's action all around.
The lifeguard is always alert.

"Watch out for that flying umbrella!"
"Got a Band-Aid?"
"Jellyfish sting!"

Back Beach
Behind the lifeguard stand.

Surfchair: A wheelchair with tires that can be pushed through soft sand and shallow water.

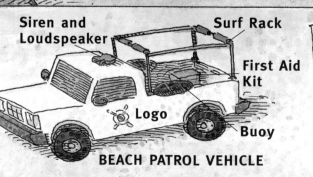

Siren and Loudspeaker

Surf Rack

First Aid Kit

Logo

Buoy

BEACH PATROL VEHICLE

MOST COMMONLY USED CB TERMS	
10-2	Hello
10-4	Affirmative
10-7	Off Duty
10-8	On Duty
10-19	Station
10-20	Location
10-95	Lost Child

"Thief!"

"I'm lost!"

"It's my raft, not yours!"

"Land emergency! Possible heatstroke! Get the medic! Start CPR!"

Jellyfish
Vinegar may relieve the sting.

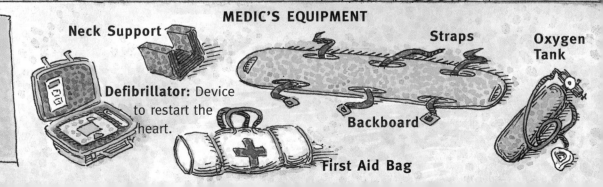

MEDIC'S EQUIPMENT

Neck Support

Defibrillator: Device to restart the heart.

Straps

Oxygen Tank

Backboard

First Aid Bag

...dangerous surfing

...boating near bathers

...playing ball, horseshoes,
and other sports too close
to others' space

...littering

...sand throwing

...drinking alcohol

BEACH RULES

- Listen to the lifeguards
- Respect others around you
- For a safe and fun day at the beach there should be **no**...

...unattended children

...diving head-first in shallow water

HELP!

...horseplay

...fishing in bathing area

...loud music

...feeding gulls

...dogs on the loose

WHISTLE SIGNALS

Long: *tweeeeeeeeeeeee*—Attention
Moderate: *tweeeee*—Stand By
Short: *twee, twee, twee*—Rescue

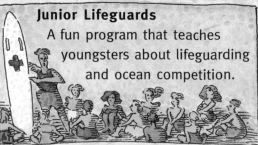

Junior Lifeguards
A fun program that teaches youngsters about lifeguarding and ocean competition.

HELP!

Uh-oh! Someone is caught in a rip. GET READY! Alert the other stands. **RESCUE!**

Short whistles, hats and sunglasses flying, lifeguards jumping, running!

GO!

GO!

GO!

GO!

TWEE TWEE TWEE

Rip Current Facts

- A rip current is a strong flow formed on the water's surface as waves return to the sea after breaking on shore.
- If caught in a rip, swim parallel to shore until you escape, or float until help arrives.

Bottlenose Dolphin

The beach patrol guards react as a team. They dash, porpoise, and stroke to the victim. "Don't panic!" "Stay calm!" "Grab the torp!"

Other lifeguards on the beach will "cover up" the empty stands while a rescue is in action.

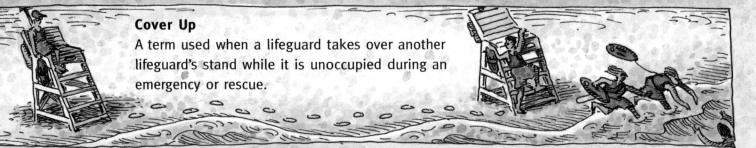

Cover Up
A term used when a lifeguard takes over another lifeguard's stand while it is unoccupied during an emergency or rescue.

The victim is now secure. It's time to form a chain.
Link up torpedoes! Swim together back to shore.

STROKE!
KICK!
STROKE!
KICK!

Porpoising
A method of moving through surf that is too deep for running but too shallow for swimming.

Run   Jump   Dive   Jump   Dive   Jump

"He's okay! Hooray!"

The crowd on the beach applauds the rescue as the victim is brought safely to shore.

The lifeguards begin to hustle back to their stands— *Whoa! What was that?*

Gullysnatch
A rescue in shallow water, usually of a small child.

Gully
An area of water between the beach and a sandbar; depending on the tide, it can be quite deep.

Reel
A line sometimes used in rescues to tow a victim to shore.

THUNDER

CLEAR THE WATER!

ICE CREAM

Boat Rescue

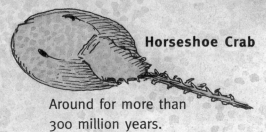

Horseshoe Crab

Around for more than 300 million years.

LIGHTNING

CLEAR THE BEACH!

UMBRELLAS
CHAIRS
FLOATS

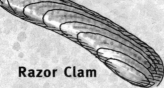

Razor Clam

Lightning Facts
- The time between lightning and its thunder is five seconds per mile.
- Lightning can strike 10 miles from a storm.

A thunderstorm is coming in fast. The sea is churning, sand is blowing, umbrellas and chairs are flying. The ocean and open beach are dangerous places to be in a storm.

When everyone is cleared to safety, the guards, too, will head for cover—*BUT WAIT!*

MY CHILD, WHERE'S MY CHILD?

SAFE PLACES TO BE IN A THUNDERSTORM

Car

Building

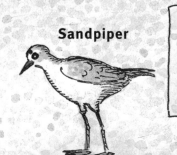

Sandpiper

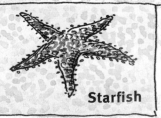

Starfish

LOST KID!

Rockweed

Lost Kid Observation #1
Lost kids usually walk with the wind at their backs.

A child is lost during all the commotion.

"10-95."
"Form a search party!"
"Calm the frantic parent!"
"Alert the police!"
"Check everywhere!"
"We're looking for a four-year-old girl in a red bathing suit.
Her name is Tess.
Brown hair,
red suit: 10-4."

SHE'S UNDER HERE.

UMBRE
CHA
FLO

Lost Kid Observation #2
Lost kids usually walk in one direction and rarely go back the other way.

Herring Gull

***P**hew!* The storm blows by, and there's a happy reunion. The lifeguards set back up as bathers return to enjoy the rest of the day.

At 5:30 P.M., the guards clear the water. This warns the bathers that they are about to go off duty. With people safely on shore, the "knock-off" signal goes down the beach and the guards drag their stands back to the soft sand. Now it's time to head for the tent.

LIFEGUARD RACES TONIGHT

Skate Eggs

Skate

Helpful Hints
- Only swim near a lifeguard.
- Remember your "street" name or a nearby landmark.
- Always stay near a familiar adult.
- If you get lost, tell a lifeguard.

KNOCK OFF

COMPETITORS TAKE YOUR MARK ...

Common Mussels

Before knock-off, a "clear-the-water" signal is given to tell bathers to come back to shore.

Snowy Egret

PADDLEBOARD

But this beach day is not over for the patrol.

As the sun sets, lifeguard races begin—swimming, running, dashing, rowing, and paddling.

Beach patrols from nearby towns come to test their skills, to the delight of the crowd.

SWIM

...GO!

RACE OFFICIALS

Timer

Judges

Starter

Tillering (or **Tilling**)
Using an oar to "steer" the boat.

SURF DASH

SINGLES ROW

TWO MILE RUN

Pitchpoling: To cause the boat to flip end over end.

Waverunner

RACE FLAG

Cinder Block

Anchor Line

Buoy

As lifeguard victors walk up the tent ramp to receive their trophies, whistles blow and the winners celebrate. It's 8:30 P.M. and time to pack up.

For the guards, it is all about saving and protecting lives— what they do best.

Another typical day for the beach patrol comes to an end.